SEE WHAT I MEAN?
A Collection of Poems

by

LLOYD KEMP

ISBN: 978-1-905795-77-2

Published by Aspect Design
and printed and bound at their premises
89 Newtown Road, Malvern, WR14 1PD

Acknowledgements

I am indebted to my friend Dorothy for the cover photograph, which began life as a snapshot taken during a visit from Australia with her husband Bruce, to whom I am equally indebted for many discussions concerning the lay-out and content of this book.

Likewise, I am deeply grateful to my friends Barry and Maureen, for their continued help and encouragement at all times.

Finally, it is a great pleasure to record my grateful thanks to my friend Marian, who undertook the onerous task of reading the whole manuscript from cover to cover in search of typographical errors.

Preface

It will be seen from the list of Contents which follows, that the poems have been assembled in the alphabetical order of their titles. At first sight this may seem to be rather arbitrary. However, as the reader's acquaintance with the poems grows, it will be realized that their subject matter is wide-ranging – from the light-hearted and distinctly quirky, to those concerned with some of the deepest aspects of this human life of ours.

So, often, the next poem will come as something of a surprise. And that's how I like it! – after all, Life itself is full of surprises, isn't it?

Lloyd Kemp, Bath, 2011

Contents

Prologue

------------ See What I mean...? ------------

'You see – being old
is a responsibility.'

'You mean –
for the people
taking care of you.'

'No – for *me!*'

'How so?'

'Well, you know –
people tend to
take their cue from
oldies like me:
they look at you
out of the corner
of their eye, and
(depending on
what they see),
they think, either
that being old
isn't as bad as
it's made out
to be, or they
mutter under
their breath, "If
it's as bad as *that,*
then put me down
for dying young,
or at least before
old age has got its
hands on me."
See what I mean,
about responsibility?'

'I do. But
I have to say
you seem to be
making a go
of it.'

'That's because
I'm in my second
childhood.'

'You're *what?*'

'You see – I've lost
the blasé-ness
of youth and
middle age, and
regained a sense
of wonder.'

'Is that *all?*"

'It's everything.
Well – *al*-most...

And stop looking
at me out of
the corner of
your eye.'

A Change in the Weather

A friend brought me
flowers: they were
daffodils.

It was late,
on a dull, dark
February afternoon,
the flowers tight-shut –
refusing (it seemed)
to have any truck
with the bleakness
all about them.

Overnight, they
slept, nestled up
to one another
in a vase brimful,
not just of water,
but of joy – the joy
of being rescued
from the dark recesses
of a kitchen cupboard,
and chosen to fill
the supporting role
to such bright stars
as a host of golden
daffodils.

The next morning
it was even duller,
and raining, but
the daffodils –
relenting –
had opened
their hearts to
the world: yes! –

despite the rain
and the slate-grey sky,
the *sun* was out –

and out to stay.

A Question of Terminology

Late afternoon, and a
knock at the door:
it was the postman –
but no letter.

'Sorry, sir.
I dropped it
down a drain.'

'You *what?*'

'Yes, sir.'

'Was it a *real* one?
I mean – address
handwritten, and an
honest-to-goodness
stamp.'

'Yes, sir.
But not to
worry your head.
I'll borrow a
pair o' them tongs
like folk use for
picking things up
off the floor. But
pray it don't rain
till I'm back again!'
And off he went.

A second knock,
and there he was,
this time all smiles,
and clutching a
letter – besmirched,
but hand-written,
in a *lady's* hand!

What a good thing
it hadn't got lost
'in the post'! –

or should I have said,
'down a drain'?

----------- **Age Matters** ----------

Old age
is, at present,
centre stage,
if BBC News,
and the columns
of the dailies are
anything to go by.

First, and foremost
are the politicians,
many of whom
(so it would seem)
see old age as
little more than
dying in slow motion;
and legislate,
accordingly.

As well, there are
the local authorities,
who complain that
they it is who have
"to foot the bill" –
a way of putting it
befitting the more
mundane of their
responsibilities
(such as clearing
the streets of
rubbish).

And not to be
overlooked are
the scientists who
hit the headlines:
responding to an
intellectual challenge,
as they strive to add
to our life-span,
in the face of a
society which is
failing to keep pace
with them.

Last, but by
no means least,
are those involved
in a personal way –
the ageing one a
father or mother,
uncle, aunt or
who-so ever;
theirs the harshest
of dilemmas:

naturally desirous of
the best for Mum or
Dad, or Aunt or Uncle
So-and-So, but –

what if the cost
should stretch,
way beyond
their means?

We *could* go on:
the treatment of
the agéd in many a
so-called "Care Home"
a travesty of caring,
and so on, and so on,
ad nauseam;

but –
this culture of ours
having already made
a dog's breakfast
of the matter –
it would seem
pointless to
say more:

except –
ah, yes – to
remind ourselves
that, in so-called
'primitive' societies,
old age is not a
problem to be
feared, but a
stage in life,

to be revered.

And The Answer?

Sometimes, we feel
a need for help, if
we're to go on living
in this world of ours,
with its limited answers
to an unlimited number
of questions.

Or should we accept that
there are some questions
for which the appropriate
answer is 'No answer.'? -
an invitation to cease
asking the question;

to be free, then, to
feel the wonder,
evoked by the
unanswerable.

At first light

I sat, quietly
contemplating
the horizon, as –
for another day –
it resumed its role
of meeting place of
Earth and sky.

And, as I
watched, the sky –
already pale yellow –
deepened to gold,
the sky above it
to yellow-green;
and, above that,
to a daytime
azure blue.

It was
as though God
were saying to me,
'Nothing more is
required, than that
you sit, watch, and
wait, and my glory
shall surely be
revealed –

and that shall
ever be.'

------------ **Be Still — and Know** ------------

It was Elijah
who discovered
that when God
had something
to say to him,
he didn't bellow,
in the manner of
a Force Nine gale,
nor did he take him
by the shoulders
and shake him, with
the violence of
an earthquake of
strength Seven on
the Richter Scale;
nor speak in a
tone of voice as
heated as a
forest fire.

No – he spoke in
'a still small voice' –
'a soft whispering
murmur', as my
Concordance has it.

But isn't that rather
out of character for a
God supposedly
omnipotent?
Surely a gale, or
an earthquake, or
a raging fire
would have been
more likely to
impress. So –
why the whisper?

Could it be that
not even God is
prepared to
compete with the
left-brain babble
we tolerate,
day long? –
the willingness
to switch it off
a *sine qua non,*
if we are to have
any chance at all
of hearing what he
has to say.

And the
'still small voice'
makes quite sure
we *do* just that.

Be Still — and Go!

It was early morning –
pre-washing, pre-shaving,
pre-breakfast time –
as I endeavoured
to be still, not simply
in body, but in mind and
spirit too, with waves
of left-brain activity
already assailing
the peaceful shore-line
of the new day.

Then it was that –
in my mind's eye –
I saw a vision of
Christ, calming the
storm-tossed waves
of a raging sea.

And –
immediately –
the sea along the
shore-line of my day
became 'as calm as
a millpond' – with
its latent energy to
power the wheel
on which the new
day would later
turn.

Beauty Has Many Faces

A volcano coughs,
and its death-dealing
sputum destroys a
neighbouring city;
whilst its trouble-laden
breath, inhaled by
aircraft engines, can
ground flights a
continent away.

Yet,
in the
very infliction
of destruction
on such scale
does it display
an awesome
beauty - laden

with death.

Bud of Life

Could we
but apprehend
the full wonder
of the miracle
we call 'Life',
then would all
that comes to us
be seen – 'good'
and 'bad' alike –
as the unfolding
of a bud, in the
face, oft-times,
of inclement
weather; yet set
ultimately to
attain the full
beauty of the
blossom.

Cart Before Horse

No –
it's not *our* Planet,
though we treat it
as though it were:
it was loaned to us
by the Landlord
rent-free, terms
and conditions
applying,
aeons ago.

Yet –
were someone to
treat the albeit lifeless
bricks and mortar of
our house and home
with the same blatant
disregard we mete out
to Planet Earth, it would
have us choking
apoplectically.

Christmas Perspective

On a long walk,
to arrive at a stile
is to be given
the time to take stock:
a time of retrospect
and anticipation,
a time to look back
over the way we have
come, and forward,
to the way ahead –
with all its promise.

So, too, arriving at
Christmas, with the
difference that, unlike
the dead timbers
of the stile, Christmas
lives! –

and will share
its Life with us all,

if we but
let it.

**Comparisons,
Far From Odious**

Second only
to a sunny day,
the magic of
a moonlit night.

Second only
to the bird
in flight, the
bird on song,
at break of day.

Second only
to a child
at play, the
play of light on
salt sea's spray.

And, second only
to the gift of
love, the gift
of laughter
shared.

Daffodil Days

Severed from
Mother Earth,
that had given
birth to them,
the daffodils
were like children
deprived access
to their mother's
milk; a mere
three times two
days plus one, their
life expectancy:

Day One, and
no evidence
that time had
anything at all
to say to them:
a childhood,
spent simply
enjoying
what it is to
be alive.

Day Two, and
still not on
speaking terms
with time: filled
with the wonder
of being daffodils,
their bright-yellow
petals outstretched,
to emulate the sun,
their golden trumpets
held high, as if to
sound the praise of
daffodils, worldwide.

Day Three,
and time still
trying to get a
word in edgeways –
the daffodils
in their prime:
heads high, stems
straight, their faces
bright as the
midday sun:
why *shouldn't*
life just go on
and on?

It was Day Four
when, at last,
time managed to
make itself heard –
but, in no more than
a whisper: did I
see just a *hint*
of a wrinkle
round the mouths
of those trumpets
of supposedly
everlasting
gold? And those
wide-armed,
yellow petals,
endeavouring
to embrace the
world: were they
looking just that
little bit less
youthful-
fresh?

Day Five, and
and there was
no denying it:
time, at long last,
had had its say;
stems – like spinal
columns – bent at
the shoulders,
the flower-heads
crowning them
no longer skyward-
looking for their
inspiration,
but – somewhat
disconsolately –
staring at
the floor.

Day Six – the
march of time
inexorable now –
and old age
come to stay.
From now on,
would not the
kind of care
involved be
more like a
burden – not only
for me, but
for the daffodils
themselves?

My hand was round
the bundle of
slightly-sagging
stems; the heads that
topped them drooping
still more sadly now,
as if responding to
a mystical awareness
that society-writ-large
had already decided
on their fate.
I looked again –
a look that began
with a 'sorry-but-it's-
all-for-the-best' intent,
but ending in a shame-
faced lowering of eyes.

But then – *just* then –
I found myself
putting the daffodils
back again, in a
vase fresh-filled
with life-sustaining
water. It's true, it
wrought no miracle:
the wrinkles round
those golden-trumpet
mouths ever-deepening;
the bright sunshine-
yellow petals
abandoning
their ambition
to embrace the
Universe, and
settling for
simple survival.

Day Seven, and
high privilege it was,
to have them share
their old age with me;
the heart-warming
gold and yellow
of their faces still
redolent with the
glimpse of the heaven
that lay about them
in their infancy –

a glimpse on-going,
which would have been
lost in the provisions
made for agéd daffodils,
to which I had all but
committed them:

my compost heap.

Dicing With Disaster

Millions
envied them – but
across a gulf which
they were powerless
to narrow, much as
they longed to do so;
the yawning chasm
opening up in
no more time than
it took to dial a
telephone number,
or access the
Internet: yes! –
just that.

And as for the
object of such
covetousness,
no celebrities, they! –
if you'd met them
in the street the
day before, it would
certainly not have
prompted you to
turn your head, or
even bat an eyelid.

That said, as I
listened to their
near-hysteric
chatter, I was
assailed by doubt
on their behalf:
they thought they
were riding high,
but, already, were
they floundering;
and pity, then,
began to replace
doubt.

For – as sure as
night follows day –
just round the corner
from their gleefulness
potential disaster
lurked; and their
chatter started to
acquire a nervous
edge, as they
caught a glimpse
of the pitfalls that
awaited them.

As for *myself* –

I was swamped
by a wave of
thankfulness: that
at any rate *my* life
would go on, as it
had ever done.

But – for *them?*

Indeed –
for them I
felt naught but
deep concern: that –
unwittingly –
they had risked
being consumed by
the soul-destroying
anxieties of having
to manage a fortune
of tens of millions
of pounds –

wished on them,
as it were by the
roll of a ball - yes -

in the Lottery.

Easter Thought

Most of us have
been heard to say –
of what has already
happened – 'It's
un-believable!'

And isn't that
how it is – with
Christ's death,
and resurrection?

Evolving Thoughts, on Evolution

Just suppose
there was a
second 'Big Bang' –
no – not to create
another Universe,
but something
equally significant –
Man:

no sign of him –
and then, in a
trillionth of a
second, he
finds himself
on Planet Earth:
body, mind and spirit –
a whole human being,
but as from nowhere,
and alone.
How, and what,
would he feel?

Post-traumatic stress?

I guess so.

But *that*
pre-supposes
awareness of
a self, able to
feel the stress.
So – *who* would he
think he was?

Equipped
with a memory,
but nothing to
remember, and,
without roots
nourished by
a past, he'd surely
find himself in an
identity crisis,
hard on the heels
of post-traumatic
stress – and all
down to a Creator
devoid of empathy
with his creation.

But –
what of a
Creator who *had*
such empathy?
Would he not wish
to spare Man
the trauma of
instantaneous
creation?

In fact,
wouldn't it be
precisely
what we know as
evolution that
he would choose,
to create
homo sapiens?

So -
is *that* why,
with Earth itself
four and a half
billion years old,
a billion of them
had elapsed
before there was
any *sign* of life;
with *homo sapiens*
appearing some
three billion years
later still: a mere
half *million* years
ago?

Is *that* how long
the Creator took,
not simply to give
Darwin something
to think about, but
to ensure that Man
was no mere puppet? –
equipping him
with heart, soul and
mind that would
come to create
great art, great music,
and great literature,
reflecting the glory
of the Creator:

his beauty, his
joy, his peace, and
his all-embracing
love for his
Creation.

Food for Thought

Mostly,
what we buy for
our consumption has
a "Best Before" date.

Again,
we sometimes say
(of an idea),
"I'll buy that."

And I
wondered:
do the *ideas* we 'buy'
have a "Best Before"
date, too?

Or,
for some,
against "B B",
does it simply say,
"Not Applicable"? –
the truth they
embody, of a
kind that lasts
for ever:

no "Best Before",
but *surely* a
"Best Buy"?

Gain, *Without* Pain!

Within sight of
what some might call
its "Use By" date,
my body, I find, in
increasing need of
attention:

a knee, an ankle,
a wrist, or whatever —
each the worse
for wear (or tear) and
a burden, growing
day by day.

At least, that's how it
had seemed to me.

But then,
quite suddenly —
in the middle of
the near-ritualistic
application of
ointment, liniment,
or moisturizing cream —
it came to me
that this was no
tiresome chore, but
more, *much* more:
none less than the
means whereby
I would be able to
live my life for a
whole new day,
unmarred by
needless
pain:
gain indeed, and
without pain —

no small thing,
at ninety-seven!

Growth Solves Everything –
Or Does It?

Babies know
they need to
grow: it's written
on their genes.
They also know
(the source the same)
that time will come
when it has to
cease.

It's the same
with elephants:
big as they get,
they never forget
that to grow still more
would be a hindrance
rather than a
help.

Likewise, giraffes:
after aeons of
trial and error
concluding that
longer necks
would be a
liability -
rather than
an asset.

And as for the
giant redwoods:
they had their reasons
for stopping feet short
of four hundred –
which is just as well:
with but finite source
of sustenance,
'the sky's the limit'
just not on.

Economists
and politicians
look the other way
when it comes to
what babies
know from birth,
and elephants
never forget –
not to mention
what the giraffe
found out, about
heads in clouds, or
the giant redwoods'
ill-fated attempt
to reach for
the sky.

'Growth'
is the buzzword
of the day, though
fuzzword would be
nearer the truth —
'five per cent
per annum'
the magic number
bandied about.

Involving a
like increase
in consumption of
resources, this
(as every schoolboy —
even in Macaulay's day—
would know) demands
a *doubling,* every
score of y*ea*rs.
And — generous
as Mother Earth
may be — she will
waste no time in
letting it be known
that *that* is
unsustainable.

But, plain as the
proverbial pikestaff
though it be - to babies,
elephants and giraffes -
beware! Who knows
which way the wind
blows, in the mind
of a self-serving
economist, or
a vote-hungry
politician?

Heaven on Earth?

These days,
we prefer to
speak in terms
of the abstract:
of 'the Spirit',
and 'the Light':
less often do we
mention
God.

It's odd,
is it not? –
for *that* would
really bring us
nearer Heaven;

and,
at the same time,
down to Earth.

Could *that* be
the *problem?*

Horizons – and Beyond

We think of the horizon
as the line dividing
earth from sky;
but of much greater
significance, its role
as the far point of our
vision, beyond which,
a whole Universe –
extending (as they say)
'to infinity'.

Symbolized
by a figure '8'
lying on its side
(an *endless* loop?)
'infinity' is, in truth,
a mathematical
abstraction, where
parallel straight lines
are yet said to meet.

But such concept
of 'infinity' –
as a *location* –
neatly sidesteps
the challenge to
both head and heart,
involved in stating
the reality: that the
Universe extends
'infinitely', and that
parallel straight lines,
in fact, *never* meet.

'That's just a quibble,'
did I hear you say?

Far from it: with
our lives lived in
finite terms – of
length, breadth, height,
and time – we are
unable even to *conceive*
of the immeasurable:
that we live, move, and
have our being at a
point in so-called 'space'
to which – in whatsoever
direction we choose to look –
there is *no* end.

In fact,
we live in 'a
riddle wrapped in a
mystery inside an
enigma'. What bathos
then! – to denote it
by a mere symbol, and,
as well, to speak of it
as a place where
parallel straight lines
meet up – yet they
don't. So – let's face it:
there's no such *place*
as 'Infinity'.

But there's
plenty of *space* – for
the Child in us

to *wonder* at it all.

Hunches – and HUNCHES

As a scientist,
all too familiar am I
with the problem
which, long since,
has ceased to be
the latest challenge
on which to sharpen
my scientific wits,
to become, instead,
the ghost which nightly
haunts me long after
I've sought refuge in the
comfort of my bed –
and waiting, night-long,
to wreck the peace
of my awakening.

Yet, as well,
do I know the
excitement of
the heady hunch,
promising
an answer to
a problem which
had beset me for
(seemingly) a
near-lifetime.

Yet,
is such hunch
as *nothing,*
compared with
the hunch which –

with the doors of
heart and mind
flung wide in
contemplation –

comes, like a
lightning flash,
to illuminate both
the outer spaces
of the Universe, and
the inner spaces
of the soul.

Identity Crisis

We need to stay
within ourselves:

if we step outside,
we risk others
seeing us as
someone else.

And back inside again,
beware! – lest we fail
to take the coat off
which we put on when
we went outside.

Immanuel

At break of day,
I prayed for
God to be with me,
every step of
the way.

But,
it was
given me then,
that my real need
was for a day-long
awareness that
that was ever
and always
so.

Information Tempt-ology

When I surf the Net
I expect to get wet, in
a shower of information,
but I strongly object
to being drenched by
a downpour of tempting
advertisements.

Life –
After Death

The marguerites –
at home, in their
earthenware pot –
had adorned my
table for a full
three weeks:
heads held high,
and smiling
sweetly,
whenever I
passed by.

With catastrophic
suddenness then, they
bowed their heads –
pleading with me that
they be allowed to
die in the fresh air,
under a clear-blue sky.

And I granted them
their wish.

But, Creator-god
had other plans for his
creation: raining on them
tears of joy, and warming
their hearts with sun-
beamed love, he
coaxed them
back to life
again!

Living Alone

can be a bind, but
does it have to be? –
after all, in the silence,
you're free to talk
to yourself – and even
to God – with no-one
to look askance
at you;

and the back-drop
a silence akin to that
of a Quaker Meeting.
What more could I
want?

D'you know? – I
don't think I'll
attempt to answer
that one: it might
take too long.

Mist, and Mystery

The mist lay in the valley,
and I looked down on it
as on a calm white sea.
But, even as I watched,
it was dispersing —
to reveal what had
lain hidden beneath it,
moments before.

But today,
as I watched,
it happened in reverse —
the valley filling with mist,
there, before my eyes.
And, in that moment,
it seemed that God
had said, 'Yes, I
reveal, but I also
obscure.'

And then, as I
continued watching,
the sun came out —

and that which
concealed, revealed
a beauty all its own.

'My cleaner'

Yes –
many there are
who refer to her
simply as 'my cleaner',
but – for myself – I prefer
to pay the respect due
to the one who bustles in
to the untidiest of untidy
spaces that I call 'home',
with not even the hint
of a smile on its face,
to leave it – mere hour
later – grinning broadly
from bath to bed, and
lounge to larder: *'Doesn't*
that look nice?' she says,
as much to herself,
as to me.

No mere *'cleaner'* she:
to me she's 'the lady who
cleans for me' - for short,
'my cleaning lady'.

And the difference?

That's simple:
my cleaning lady
is a human being,
but my *cleaner*
could be just a
pump-spray bottle
of 'Jif'.

My Take on Bin Day

When I was young,
we used to call them
"dustmen" – like
"refuse collectors"
a euphemism for
"those who do our
dirty work for us."

But we don't
pay them any extra –
we, whose privilege
it is, to be doing
the work we *chose*
to do, not work
which chose *us.*

Did you ever
hear of a dustman
(*or* refuse collector –
call him what you will)
who expressed the hope
that he would continue as
a refuse collector for the
rest of his working days?

It's true – he *runs*
to and fro with my bin –
only too eager, it would
seem, to deal with the
fresh lot of rubbish,
awaiting him, next door.

Or could it be,
that he's on
piecework? –
motivation a
poor second-best
to a sense of
vocation, enjoyed
by the likes of
you and me:
don't you think we
owe him at least a
debt of gratitude –

and something a
little more substantial,
come next Boxing Day?

(Or is "Boxing Day", like
"Christmas": twenty-first-
century-speak, for
"Leave us alone, to
enjoy what we've got."?)

----------- My Word! ------------

I click on "Word",
and up it comes with
"Document One":
a blank screen, and
a cursor, blinking
impatiently.

'Come on! Get going!'
it seems to say, 'I've
a whole page to fill
with poetry, before
the end of day.'

'Let's get this straight,'
I say. '*You* fill
the page - *I* write
the poetry.'

'Maybe. Maybe.
But, be warned.
The time will come
when I'll write the
poetry, too.'

'Heaven forbid!'
I mutter – but
under my breath,
lest it should take
the opportunity to
stall, halfway through
the first line of my
new masterpiece.

You see – with "Delete",
"Undo", "Repeat", "Cut",
"Copy" and "Paste" – to
say nothing of "Bold" and
"Italics" – it's so much
easier, writing poetry
on a PC, than with
pen on paper (and
all that crossing-out).

But, please!
not a *word* to "Word" –
it's got a trump card
up its sleeve: 'Word has
encountered a problem,
and needs to close.
We are sorry for the
inconvenience.'

'Inconvenience?',
I splutter. 'That poem –
all but complete –
may be lost for ever
to posterity.'

(So – you see
why I say,

'Mum's the word!')

Author's Note. This whimsical poem has a strange history. First of all, I sat down at my computer to write a quite different poem, but found myself writing this one, instead. And there was a strange, real-time sequel to writing it.

My computer had been somewhat unstable, but had performed faultlessly during my morning's work, and I was sitting, contemplating a title for the poem. Suddenly, then, without any warning (such as the one referred to in the poem!), the screen went blank, the – yes, *un*-saved – poem disappearing before my eyes.

Uncharacteristically, I was trying to be 'philosophical' about the loss of a morning's work, when - the computer having rebooted itself - "Word" re-opened, *with the complete poem filling the screen again!* - just like that!

Coals of fire?!

Night Thought

On my way to bed,
I stopped to bid
"Goodnight" to the
marguerites, which,
for many days,
had blessed me
with their company –

brightening the day
with their smiles, and

lightening the dark,
were there but
merest glimmer
of light.

And abed -
immersed
in the darkness -
I lay, wondering,

'Could *I* do that?'

'Prayer',
and
Prayer

I confess to being
perturbed – even
angry – when I hear
God harangued with
what amounts to a
Job List for his day:
'Heal the sick,
strengthen the weak,
and comfort the
lonely,' and so on,
and so on. No –
I didn't say
'ad nauseam', but I
can't help feeling that,
sometimes, it must
seem that way
to God.

And it came to me
then, that even the
prayer of concern for
another can never be
a mere request
for help, but must,
as well, be
an *offering*:

of ourselves –
our love –
providing the
link between God
and the subject of
our prayer:
the channel
along which
His love will flow –
and yes, indeed –

to 'heal the sick,
strengthen the weak,
and comfort the
lonely', too.

Private Lesson

Life
is all about
commitment –
and even a
toilet roll can
teach us much,
about that:

doubt yourself for
but a split second,
concerning the
speed of the tug
required to
get yourself
that single sheet
of which you stand
in need, and you'll
end up with a
yard or more,
surplus to
requirements.

So, too, in real life:

we need to *'go for it'*,
trusting in ourselves! –

and God.

PS:

Take not umbrage,
dear reader,
that I should use
a matter of
personal hygiene
to underline a
spiritual truth.

Remember:
innocent laughter
is the language of
Heaven itself.

Question
For the New Year

To live each day
"as if your last" –
or to live it
"as if your first"?

That is the
question, and the
answer – as it
came to me –
a paradox:

live it as if
your last,

and first.

Rays that Raise Eyebrows

It's strange, isn't it? –
that the physicist
sees double, when
he looks at light.

But wait! – we
must phrase that
some other way:
we could say that,
as the physicist
sees it, light displays
all the signs of a
dual personality;
on one occasion
behaving like
high-speed pellets,
on another, like a
fast-moving 'wave-train'
(remember shaking
the end of a
skipping rope?).

Hard-headed
though he is,
the physicist is
yet prepared
to live with such
seeming downright
contradictions –

ah -
provided, that is,
that the mystery
concerns the
behaviour of
dead matter, and
not the inner
workings of Man's
living Spirit;

the one likely,
sooner or later, to
yield up its secrets
to heavy questioning
by his cherished tool,
the Scientific Method –

the other,
never:

for a scientist
deep-dyed-
in-the-wool,
too big a pill
to swallow.

Rude Awakening

Still barely awake,
I drew the curtains –
to find my attention
riveted by a lone
traffic cone, on guard
at the entrance to my
premises; its message
short, sharp, and
unmistakeable:
"Keep Out".

No more than
a mindless joke –
even so, had it, in
but a moment,
stripped me of
the joy that comes
with the dawning day,
to replace it with
a nightmare thought:
that – on the authority
of a person, or persons,
unknown – my house
and home had been
deemed a no-go area,
for my fellow humans.

And,
in that moment,
brief though it was,
I tasted life in an
ethnic minority,
socially rejected
by the host
community.

Shaggy-Dog Story

I stepped outside
my door, and
promptly muttered,
"Drat!"

You see –
every few weeks
they fail to collect
my recyclables,
and there they were,
yet again: glass bottles,
plastic this-and-that,
scrap paper, and
food waste baking
in the sun.

I rang the man
in charge, and
gently, but firmly,
spelt out
my complaint.

* * *

Mere *minutes* later,
and I was searching
high and low for
two snail-mail letters
that had gone astray.
"It's no use," I said, to
the chap I live with
(that's me), "I've put them
in the waste bin –
they've *gone:* they're
on their way… "

A nervous bleep
then, from a fast-
coagulating brain.
"Haven't you just
rung the man, to
complain that
'on their way'
they certainly
were *not?"*

* * *

I rescued all the paper
from the outside bin,
and there, indeed,
they were!

Immediately, then,
I got on the phone –
yes, *of course!* – to
thank them for
failing to collect
my waste: surely,
that was the *least*
I could do...

But,
sadly,
the line
was busy –

though –
with hindsight –
it would seem
that was
just as well:

they must have
enough crazy
people at the
other end
of the phone,
without adding
me to their list...

------------ **Silence** ------------

One *could* say that
silence, defined
by the dictionary as
"the *absence* of sound",
does not – in any
material sense –
exist.

How then is it, that
there are many *kinds*
of silence? – variously
described, and experienced
in as many different ways:

the *awkward* silence,
when conversation flags,
and finally flounders
to a halt;

the *healing* silence,
born of a refusal to
engage in a war of
wounding words,
and long-harboured
grievances are
healed;

but, sad indeed
the *sullen* silence
of one stubbornly
refusing to say,
"Sorry".

Again – there is the
silence, *pregnant with
meaning,* as follows
the performance
of great music:
as much a part of
the score as
all the sounds
that went before;

its opposite,
the *empty* silence,
from which all life –
were it ever there –
has ebbed away.

But –

sublime -
the silence
between two
lovers, when
words fail, and –
yes! –

the silence
says it all.

Sometimes We Try Too Hard!

I wrestled with a poem, but
to no avail, reluctantly
concluding that I needed to
take a holiday from
my Muse.

And –
next morning – having
herself enjoyed the break,
she sent me a whole new
poem: beginning, middle,
and end,

just like that –

for free!

Still Roadworthy

'You *could* compare me
with a vintage car:
still roadworthy, but
with minor defects,
which make the going
that bit trickier than
it used to be.

'After a night in the
garage, my engine is
sometimes difficult
to start, even then
misfiring – and *sometimes*
grinding to a halt;
the lubrication of its
big ends (*and* little ones)
by no means what it
used to be, when I
was fresh off the
production line.

'And, recently, I've
developed a creak
in my suspension,
which, I admit, folk
find disconcerting;
I confess, too, that
my indicators are
unreliable, creating
confusion as to my
intentions.

'And it's *true* –
not long ago,
I went into reverse,
when I was looking
to go forward, which
didn't do my rear end
any good at all.

'There are some, indeed,
who say that – produced
in nineteen fourteen –
I should no longer be
on the road, but cared for
in a home for 'Classic Cars'.

'But – don't forget –
I'm keen on GPS.'

'Global Positioning Systems?'

'No! –
going places still!'

----------- That's Just The *Point* -----------

'What a wonderful story! –
I mean – the birth of Mary's son.
But, when you consider
his destiny...'

'You're right. It hardly bears
thinking about.'

'And what about the
Magi, and the gifts they
brought for him?'

'I know! – *myrrh*. Wasn't that used
for embalming a *corpse?'*

'And the story about
the money changers –
tipping up their tables –
what about *that?'*

'Well –
I must say that,
in these days,
when bankers
make fortunes
trading in
toxic debts,
I rather think
I'd *fancy* that!'

'But then there's
Gethsemane, and
all that went on there.
You know – the agony
that made him
sweat *blood:*
it happens – but
so rarely that folk
don't believe
it's true.'

'I have to confess,
I'd have chosen to
sleep through that –
like the disciples did.'

'And *God* –
He lost his *son...'*

'I know –
I know –
I tell you, I
know all there *is*
to know, about
that.'

'Yes, but it was
God – not some
poor little old human,
like yourself.'

'But that's
just the *point:*
it's *true,* he's God,
yet is it in his
very *nature* to want
to *share* with us
whatever's involved
in *being*
poor,
little,
old,
and
human –

like me.'

Author's Note:
I lost my belovéd son, Roger, very suddenly, in 2005.

It's big trouble
(and who would
deny it?) when
inanimate objects
start doing
their own thing.

And you don't
have to look far
for evidence
of what I'm
beefing on about:
take my walking
sticks. Yes, I do
have *two* of them,
and *precisely*
because of what
we're talking about:
if one of them
decides to fetch up
in a place where I'd
never dream of
putting it, then there's
always the other one
to fall back on,
so to say.

Or *is* there?
D'you *know?* –
there was a time
when *both* of them
went missing –
and *overnight!*

When I went to bed,
the spare one was
where it should be,
in the corner by the
outside door –
I *swear* it was.
And the one I'd
used, just before
I climbed into bed?
No! It *wasn't* there
beside the bed –
but – guess where:

it was by the
kitchen sink.

As if I would ever
dream of leaving it
there.

And take the case
of my glasses.
The point is,
I've got *two* pairs:
one pair for distance,
the other for reading,
and both of them
are well aware that
their place is beside
my computer,
when they're
not in use.

So –
how come
I found a pair
of all places in
the *cutlery drawer?*

Don't say it!
I know what you're
thinking; and I'm
utterly *convinced*
I didn't put them
there.

But – like all good
story-tellers –
I've kept the
best (or is it the
worst?), till last.

One day, when
I was putting
my coat on, there –
in the pocket –
were *both* pairs,
and in their cases.

Don't you even
think about
telling me that
I put them there
myself, should I
need them, when
I was out;

don't you *dare...*

The Great Escape

From time to time
we need to be
'taken out of ourselves' –
or so they say, devising
many a way, deemed
to achieve just that.

   It used to be simply a
   walk in the country, or
   a stroll beside the sea;
   pleasures which
   (it would appear)
   no longer suffice to
   turn us right side
   out again.

By all accounts,
we need to 'get away',
not only from house
and home, but town
and country, too,
shaking the dust
from our feet as we
climb aboard the
budget-airline jet,
to replace dust
with sand, from the
shores of a foreign –
yes, it *has* to be
foreign –
land.

   Trouble is,
   it may be neither
   house nor home,
   nor native town, nor
   even a once-belovéd
   fatherland, from which
   we – so feverishly –
   seek to escape:

might it be –

ourselves?

The Mulberry Bush

I was prescribed some medication
for inflammation of my knee:
three tablets a day; together with
a *second* medication, to deal with
inflammation the first might
otherwise cause in my stomach,
whilst treating the inflammation
in my knee...

Curiosity prompted me to
consult the little leaflet
accompanying the medicine,
for possible side-effects of
medicine Number Two; and –
sure enough – there it was:
a real chance of *sickness and
vomiting,* with *stomach pains*
thrown in, for good measure.

So, I thought, what about
a *third* medication, to
deal with *that?* –

or would *thrice* round the
mulberry bush be once
too many – even for the
drug manufacturers?

The Passage of Time

In some ways,
it's a matter of
simple arithmetic:
add a year to my age
of ninety-seven, and
it has increased by
a mere one per cent;
add a year to the
age of a one-year-old,
and you've actually
doubled its life! –

which explains
why, for the
very old, time
seems to pass
so quickly;
whilst, for the
very young, it
hardly seems to
exist at all.

Or –
putting it
another way:
a year out of a
future measured
in decades is
no big deal;

a great slice,
nevertheless,
out of a future
of but few years:

with each and
every dawn
heralding
the gift of
what seems
little short
of a miracle:
life – yes! – *life,*
for a whole day
more!

And you count
your blessings,
rather than
your days.

The Power of Words

Strangely,
the cold weather
seems good for
poetry: almost
a poem a day,
as the snow
continues
to fall.

  Maybe it helps
  keep me warm,
  you say?

I really think
you may be
right!

D'you know? –
the human brain
consumes energy
ten times faster
than other body
parts, averaging
a hundred watts!

  So, warm-hearted, and,
  despite the weather,
  warm-headed, too –
  goodness knows
  how many words
  of poetry one
  can produce, per
  kilowatt-hour.

The Smile

I was the
happy bearer
of good news –
where only the
worst had been
expected.

And I watched, as
the truth sank in:

first, the merest
hint of a smile,
not sure that it
had any right
to be there, but
slowly mutating to
the beginnings of a
grin, taking on
a life of its own;

and – growing
in confidence
as it went – it
advanced towards
the time-honoured
goal, of linking
ear with ear.

It seemed,
in that moment, as if
the sun had emerged
from behind a cloud –

with the difference
that, whilst the sun
would have warmed
my body, the smile
had warmed the
very cockles of
my heart.

The Ultimate Answer

So,
I'm suffering, am I? –
and feeling more than
a little sorry for myself:
'Why did it have to
happen to *me?*'

'And anyway,
what have I *done*
to deserve it?'
(My next question
to the Deity).

The answer
wasn't long
in coming.

'If your concern
is with suffering – and
unjustified, at that –
then think of being
crucified, for
responding to
hate, with
love.'

Transmutation

I went to
A. and E.
as *me*, but
came away,
a Colles
fracture:

You see –
it made life
so much
simpler for
A. and E. –
to treat me
as mere
fracture,

rather than
whole
me.

Voice Of The Morning

Thank you, Lord,
for preventing me
from bursting in
on the day, like
a bull in a china
shop; instead, to
have me sitting
quietly, in the
silence marking
its beginning;

whence,
were you able
to launch me
on my day, like
a bird, taking to
the air on the
winged words
you had spoken,

as I waited
in the stillness –

which is your
Voice.

When The Company
Has Gone

How *can* I
feel alone,
when I am
a very part
of your Being:
'a branch of
your Vine',
'a limb of
your Body'? -
as John, and
Paul have it.

So, shall I
live this day:
within you,
and at peace
within myself,
when I might
otherwise have
been engulfed
by a veritable
tsunami of
loneliness.

When Time Stood Still –
(Well – *Almost*)

It's not the first
occasion that
my kitchen clock has
had something to say
about time:
I mean – apart
from telling me
what time it is,
should I consult it.

You see,
only yesterday,
when I caught its eye,
it was saying, quite
straightforwardly,
that the time was
seventeen minutes
to two – but then,
a little later,
when I looked again,
it hadn't changed
at all.

Yet,
today,
when I looked
its way again,
it was telling me
that, after all, time
hadn't stood still,
but – nevertheless –
was passing so
slowly now that
it had yet to reach
two o'clock –
with two minutes
still to go!

I lapsed into
a day-dream:
'What if the clock
were right, and a
day – from one end
to the other –
were to use up
a mere fifteen
minutes? Then,
wouldn't that mean
I'd be destined
to live a whole
hundred times
longer? *That*
would be
great!'

But,
a clock's tick later,
and I'd suffered a
change of heart:
'Thank you – but,
"No thanks," '
I said.

And I wondered
to whom it was
that I'd spoken.

Was it merely
the *clock?*

Or my
ruminating
Self?

Or -

maybe -

was it
God?

------------ **Wherein, Omnipotence?** ------------
A Poem for Good Friday

'Almighty God,'
we say, when we
pray, but where's
the evidence? –
when, seemingly
every other day,
the earth quakes,
and whole cities are
razed to the ground;
and the sea responds
with a thirty-foot
tsunami, drowning
those still clinging
to life, buried
beneath the rubble.
'Hands up! –
those who said,
"Almighty" '.

So – what
does the word
mean to us?

If the answer is,
'having the power
(and using it) to
stop all that we
deem unpleasant
from ever afflicting
us, 'then, clearly,
God is failing
to live up to the
standards we had
set for him:
brushing aside
his own.

whatever *they*
might be, we know
that they precluded
saving his own son
from the unspeakable
fate of crucifixion.

That being so –
wherein, then,
lies his power?

Christ said, 'I,
if I be lifted up,
will draw all men
unto me' – if ever
there *were* one,
an assertion of
omnipotence.
But, pinned
by four nails –
hands and feet –
to a wooden cross:
wherein, indeed,
lay his power?

Not in the sword
(his disciple
ordered to
put away
his weapon);
nor in words
laying claim to
royal status as
the source of
his authority.
(Asked by Pilate,
'Are you a king?',
he tossed the question
back at him,
with a dismissive,
'You say that I am.')
So, what *was* it
that gave a
crucified Christ
the power to
'draw all men
unto' him?

It was Love –
yes, *love* –

incarnate:

love that refused to
respond to hate
with hate, or to force,
with even greater force;

love that lay buried
with the victims of the
earthquake and tsumani –
holding them safe, in its
embrace, through
all Eternity.

"Who is my neighbour?"

The cold,
transported
on an east wind,
and dumped
outside my door,
was tantamount
to a coil of
barbed wire,
stretched across
my porch.

Then came the
snow – Nature's
way of removing
any doubt that
I was under
house arrest.

And yet,
ever attentive,
my neighbour
cleared the snow
away – from the
pavement to
my door.

Of course,
it did nothing
to shorten the
sentence that
Nature had
passed on me.
But, strangely –
in spirit –
I felt that I
was once more
linked to the
world outside,
which had
seemed to be
passing me by.

So,
thanks be,
for one who
doesn't stop at
kindly thoughts –

but turns them into
actions.

Wink of Heaven

Engrossed
in writing
a new poem,
time ceases to
exist for me.
I am neither
old, nor young,
nor even the age
I am said to be:
I am just –

quintessential
me:

a glimpse of
God's Eternity?

I owe the title of this poem to T. S. Eliot

Words Fail — but *'Why?'*

Words
are but
poor vehicles
to convey
the depths of
human love;
and I wondered –

'Why?'

And back came
the answer,
as it were, in
the twinkling
of an eye:

human love,
at its deepest,
is God's love
too –

for which
there *are*
no words.

Epilogue

Whence Truth?

Sometimes –
when I am
sitting quietly –
it comes upon me,
of a sudden, that,
'All shall be well, and
all manner of thing,
shall be well.'

And I realize that
it is not amid the
hurly-burly of a
twenty-first-century
day – awash with
information streaming
out of mobile phones,
i-pads, and the like –
that such assurance
comes, but in the
quietness of the
moment which
claims no day, year,
or even century
as its own.

Save – perhaps –
that moment in the
Thirteen Hundreds,

when the assurance
came, new-born, to
one Julian of Norwich –
her antenna tuned,
not to a radio mast
on the crown of a
hill, but to the
source of all Truth,

with a base station
deep down in the
heart of an
anchoress.